Chefs' Special

Tandoori Cuisine

Chefs' Special

Tandoori Cuisine

Compiled by Master Chefs of India

Lustre Press
Roli Books

Flavours of Tandoori Cooking

Tandoori is India's best known export, a cuisine that suits the international palate comfortably, since it is largely meat-based, lightly spiced, and easy to both cook and serve. So named because the food is cooked in a tandoor (large coal-fired oven), it is easily adaptable to the oven, the electrical grill or the microwave. Tandoori is akin to the western barbecue, but with more delicate flavours and with marinades which enhance the flavour of the principle ingredient. The process of cooking is fast and efficient, and it is only the preparation that may take a while. Tandoori food may be served as starters, or may form a part of the main course, eaten with *roomali roti*, and mint chutney.

Indian cuisine has a range and variety that is almost extraordinary, with each region contributing its own flavour. Modern Indian cooking borrows selectively from these diverse styles, assimilates and adapts them to suit the palate. The richness of Indian food, therefore continues to grow.

Indian food is usually eaten without starters, soups or courses, though in restaurants it is presented in this manner for less familiar diners. The main meal is eaten with either rice or *roti*, and includes at least one *dal*, a selection of vegetarian servings, a meat, chicken or fish, a sampling of chutneys and pickles, and yoghurt. *Papads* are served with meals, that may be sometimes accompanied by *lassi* (buttermilk). Sweets, of course, are served with almost any Indian meal. But, depending on the region, these may be served after, during or before an Indian meal. No wonder Indian food continues to surprise its serving and style almost as variable as its thousands of recipes.

Basic Preparations

Garam masala (makes 445 gm): Take 90 gm cumin *(jeera)* seeds, 70 gm black peppercorns *(sabut kali mirch)*, 75 gm black cardamom *(badi elaichi)* seeds, 30 gm fennel *(moti saunf)*, 40 gm green cardamoms *(choti elaichi)*, 30 gm coriander *(dhaniya)* seeds, 20 gm cloves *(laung)*, 20 x 2.5 cm cinnamon *(dalchini)* sticks, 20 gm mace *(javitri)* powder, 20 gm black cumin *(shah jeera)* seeds, 15 gm dry rose petals, 15 gm bay leaves *(tej patta)*, and 15 gm ginger powder *(amchur)*.

Grind all the ingredients into a fine powder and store in an airtight container. Use as required.

Ginger / Garlic (*adrak / lasan*) paste: Soak 300 gm ginger / garlic cloves overnight to soften the skin. Peel and chop roughly. Process until pulped. The pulp can be stored in an airtight container and refrigerated for 4-6 weeks.

Wholemilk fudge (*khoya*): Boil 2 lt milk in a wok *(kadhai)*. Simmer till quantity is reduced to half, stirring occasionally. Continue cooking, now stirring constantly and scraping from the sides, till a thick paste-like consistency is obtained (1-1½ hrs.). Allow to cool.

Mint chutney: Take 60 gm mint (*pudina*) leaves, chopped, 120 gm green coriander (*hara dhaniya*), chopped, 5 gm cumin (*jeera*) seeds, 2 garlic (*lasan*) cloves, chopped, 1 green chilli, chopped, 30 gm raw mango, chopped, 45 gm tomatoes, chopped, and salt to taste.

Blend all the ingredients until paste-like. Refrigerate in an airtight container. Use as required.

Cottage cheese (*paneer*): In a pot, boil 3 lt milk. Just before it comes to the boil, add 6 tbsp lemon juice / vinegar to curdle the milk. Strain the curdled milk through a muslin cloth, to allow all whey and moisture to drain. Still wrapped in the muslin, place the cottage cheese under a weight for 2-3 hours to allow to set into a block which can be cut or grated.

Brown onion paste: Take 2 onions, chopped and 2 tbsp / 30 ml refined oil for frying.

Fry the onions over medium heat till brown. Drain excess oil and allow to cool. Process until pulped (using very little water, if required). Refrigerate in an airtight container. Use as required.

Spices – The Sweet and Sour of Indian Food

The secret of Indian cuisine lies in its spices. Used lightly but in exciting combinations, they can leave the palate tingling for more, without actually taking a toll on ones digestion.

As the story goes, the West had discovered and traded with pockets of the Indian subcontinent, primarily for its rich spices.

Although, the beneficial uses of spices have been recorded in ancient treatises, but the usage has known to vary from region to region. Apart from making food palatable, spices also have inherent cooling and warming properties. They are added to the foods intended for pregnant women, for invalids, for the old and of course, for the very young, to aid recovery or to impart stamina.

The basic Indian spices alongwith salt, are cumin (*jeera*) seeds to impart fragrance to food, turmeric (*haldi*) powder to give colour, and red chilli to spice up the food. Dry mango powder (*amchur*) adds

Turmeric powder

Red chillies

Mango powder

Asafoetida

Coriander powder

piquancy and a mere pinch of asafoetida *(hing)* adds a unique taste and also aids digestion. Fresh green coriander *(hara dhaniya)* is the most common garnish and also adds a light fragrance.

Since fruits are seen as energy-giving, dried fruits are used extensively in India. Parts of fruits, berries or vegetables are dried and stored, as condiments. Several seeds too are used, each with a marked taste.

Fennel *(moti saunf)* is added to desserts and some vegetarian dishes to act as a flavouring agent. Fenugreek seeds *(methi dana)* gives a touch of bitterness, onion seeds *(kalonji)* is used in heavier cooking or for pickles. Mustard seeds *(rai)* adds sourness to food while poppy seeds *(khus khus)* enhances the flavour of meat. Fresh tamarind *(imli)* imparts a sour taste and saffron *(kesar)*, India's most expensive herb, imparts a fine fragrance alongwith a rich yellow colour.

That Indian spices can be used almost in any fashion and to enhance any taste, is obvious from the fact that Indian tea too uses spices!! Green cardamom *(choti elaichi)* is added to tea for flavouring, while saffron and almonds are added to *kahwa* (Kashmiri tea).

Fenugreek seeds

Mustard seeds

Poppy seeds

Green cardamoms

Cloves

Murg Bannu Kebab

Delicate chicken kebab with a hint of fenugreek

Preparation time: 45 min.
Cooking time: 20 min.
Serves: 4

Chicken

Ingredients:

Chicken, cut into boneless cubes, washed, dried	900 gm
Salt	2 tsp / 8 gm
Dry fenugreek (*kasoori methi*) powder	1 tsp / 2 gm
Ginger-garlic (*adrak-lasan*) paste	2 tbsp / 36 gm
Green chillies, chopped	2 tsp
Green coriander (*hara dhaniya*), chopped	1 tbsp / 4 gm
Vinegar (*sirka*)	1 tsp / 5 ml
Refined oil	5 tbsp / 75 ml
Gram flour (*besan*), sieved	5 tsp / 15 gm
Breadcrumbs, fresh	2½ tbsp / 37 gm
Egg yolks, whisked	6

Method:

1. Mix salt, dry fenugreek powder, ginger-garlic paste, green chillies, green coriander, and vinegar; rub into the chicken. Refrigerate for 15 minutes.
2. Heat the oil in a pan; stir-fry the gram flour till a pleasing smell emanates. Add chicken cubes and sauté on low heat for 3-5 minutes till half cooked.
3. Add breadcrumbs and mix well. Remove and spread on a clean table top to cool.
4. Skewer the cubes 2" apart and roast in a tandoor till done. Bring the cubes close together and coat with egg yolks. Roast till the egg coating turns golden brown. Remove, garnish with onion rings and serve hot with mint chutney (see p. 7).

Murg Afghani Kebab
Chicken kebab flavoured with cheese

Preparation time: 4½ hrs.
Cooking time: 15 min.
Serves: 4-5

Chicken

Ingredients:

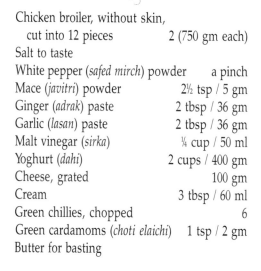

Chicken broiler, without skin, cut into 12 pieces	2 (750 gm each)
Salt to taste	
White pepper (*safed mirch*) powder	a pinch
Mace (*javitri*) powder	2½ tsp / 5 gm
Ginger (*adrak*) paste	2 tbsp / 36 gm
Garlic (*lasan*) paste	2 tbsp / 36 gm
Malt vinegar (*sirka*)	¼ cup / 50 ml
Yoghurt (*dahi*)	2 cups / 400 gm
Cheese, grated	100 gm
Cream	3 tbsp / 60 ml
Green chillies, chopped	6
Green cardamoms (*choti elaichi*)	1 tsp / 2 gm
Butter for basting	

Method:

1. Mix salt, white pepper, ½ tsp mace powder, ginger and garlic pastes with malt vinegar. Rub the mixture into chicken and marinate for 1 hour.
2. Mix the remaining ingredients (except butter) together. Transfer the marinated chicken into this yoghurt mixture. Keep aside for 3 hours.
3. Preheat the oven to 180°C / 350°F. Skewer the chicken pieces, 2 cm apart. Keep a tray underneath to collect the drippings. Roast in an oven / tandoor / grill for 10-12 minutes. Remove and hang the skewers to allow the excess marinade to drip off.
4. Baste with butter and roast for 3 more minutes.
5. Serve hot with lemon wedges and naan or roti.

Murg Paneer Tikka

Chicken tikka marinated in cottage cheese

Preparation time: 4 hrs.
Cooking time: 15 min.
Serves: 4-6

Ingredients:

Chicken breasts, cut into boneless cubes	1 kg
Lemon (*nimbu*) juice	1 tbsp / 15 ml
Garlic (*lasan*) paste	3 tbsp / 54 gm
Salt to taste	
Cottage cheese (*paneer*), grated	150 gm
Cream	4 tbsp / 80 ml
Cornflour	1½ tbsp / 15 gm
Green chilli paste	2 tsp / 10 gm
White pepper (*safed mirch*) powder	1 tsp / 2 gm
Green coriander (*hara dhaniya*), chopped	1 tbsp / 4 gm
Butter for basting	

Method:

1. Marinate chicken in lemon juice, garlic paste, and salt mixture for 1 hour.

2. Mix cottage cheese, cream, cornflour, green chilli paste, white pepper powder, and green coriander in a bowl; whisk till smooth. Marinate chicken in this mixture for at least 3 hours.

3. Skewer chicken 2 cm apart and roast in a preheated (180°C / 350°F) oven / tandoor / grill for 8-10 minutes. Baste with butter and roast for another 3 minutes or until golden in colour.

4. Garnish with tomato, onion, and cucumber slices and serve hot with mint chutney (see p. 7).

Murg Malai Tikka
Creamy chicken tikka

Preparation time: 3 hrs. 45 min.
Cooking time: 12 min.
Serves: 4-6

Chicken

Ingredients:

Chicken breasts, cut into boneless cubes	1 kg
Garlic (*lasan*) paste	2 tbsp / 36 gm
Ginger (*adrak*) paste	2 tbsp / 36 gm
Salt to taste	
White pepper (*safed mirch*) powder	1 tsp / 2 gm
Egg, whisked	1
Cheddar cheese, grated	60 gm
Green chillies, deseeded, finely chopped	8
Green coriander (*hara dhaniya*), finely chopped	1 cup / 25 gm
Mace-nutmeg (*javitri-jaiphal*) powder	½ tsp
Cornflour	1 tbsp / 10 gm
Cream	¾ cup / 150 ml
Refined oil / Butter for basting	

Method:

1. Rub garlic-ginger pastes, salt, and white pepper into the chicken cubes. Keep aside for 15 minutes.
2. Mix the remaining ingredients together (except oil / butter); coat the chicken with this prepared mixture. Marinate for at least 3 hours.
3. Skewer the chicken cubes 2 cm apart and roast in a preheated (140°C / 275°F) oven / grill / tandoor for 5-8 minutes. Hang the skewers for 3-5 minutes to allow excess marinade to drip off; brush with oil and roast again for 3 minutes.
4. Garnish with green coriander, tomato slices, and lemon wedges and serve hot with mint chutney (see p. 7).

Tangri Kebab
Chicken drumsticks coated with cashew batter

Preparation time: 1 hr.
Cooking time: 15-20 min.
Serves: 4

Ingredients:

Chicken, drumsticks	12
Ginger-garlic (*adrak-lasan*) paste	4 tsp / 24 gm
White pepper (*safed mirch*) powder	a pinch
Salt	1 tsp / 4 gm
Vinegar (*sirka*)	1 tsp / 5 ml
Yoghurt (*dahi*)	1¼ cups / 250 gm
Cream	¾ cup / 150 gm
Ginger-garlic paste	2 tbsp / 36 gm
White pepper powder	1 tsp / 2 gm
Garam masala (see p. 6)	2 tsp / 4 gm
Salt	½ tsp / 2 gm
Saffron (*kesar*)	a few strands
Refined oil for basting	
Eggs, whisked	4
Cashew nuts (*kaju*), finely ground	5 tbsp / 75 gm

Method:

1. Wash and clean the chicken drumsticks. Make 4-5 deep vertical incisions.
2. Mix ginger-garlic paste, white pepper powder, salt, and vinegar together. Coat the drumsticks with this paste and rub into the slits. Refrigerate for 15 minutes.
3. Make a second marinade with yoghurt, cream, ginger-garlic paste, white pepper powder, garam masala, salt, and saffron.

Chicken

Chicken

4. Marinate the chicken in the prepared marinade and refrigerate for another 15 minutes.
5. Skewer the drumsticks and roast in a tandoor for 3-5 minutes till half cooked. Remove and hang for 2-3 minutes to allow the excess marinade to drip off.
6. Baste with oil / butter and roast till completely cooked.
7. Mix the cashew nut paste and eggs together. Coat the drumsticks with this batter and roast again till the egg has coagulated. Remove from skewers.
8. Serve hot with mint chutney (see p. 7).

Perk it up!
If the yoghurt is sour,
add a little fresh milk.

Chukandri Tangri Kebab

Chicken drumsticks with beetroot

Preparation time: 3 hrs.
Cooking time: 20 min.
Serves: 4-5

Ingredients:

Chicken drumsticks, without skin	15

For the first marinade:

Beetroot (*chukandar*), finely grated	150 gm
Lemon (*nimbu*) juice	2 tbsp / 30 ml
Salt to taste	

For the second marinade:

Yoghurt (*dahi*), whisked	¾ cup / 150 gm
Black cumin (*shah jeera*) seeds	2 tsp / 4 gm
Cream	4 tbsp / 80 ml
Garam masala (see p. 6)	2 tsp / 4 gm
Ginger (*adrak*) paste	2 tbsp / 36 gm
Garlic (*lasan*) paste	2 tbsp / 36 gm
Butter for basting	4 tsp / 20 gm

Method:

1. Make 2 deep incisions on each drumstick.
2. Mix all ingredients of first marinade and rub evenly over chicken legs. Marinate for 1 hour.
3. Mix all ingredients of second marinade. Marinate chicken in this mixture; refrigerate for 2-3 hours.
4. Preheat oven to 180°C / 350°C. Skewer the drumsticks, leaving a gap of at least 2 cm. Keep a tray underneath to collect the drippings.
5. Roast in hot tandoor / oven / grill for about 10-15 minutes. Baste continuously with butter. Garnish with lemon wedges and parsley and serve hot on a bed of shredded cabbage.

Neza Kebab

Chicken drumsticks flavoured with green cardamom

Preparation time: **40** min.
Cooking time: **25** min.
Serves: **4**

I n g r e d i e n t s :

Chicken, drumsticks — 900 gm
For the marinade:
Ginger-garlic (*adrak-lasan*)
  paste — 5 tbsp / 90 gm
Salt — 1½ tsp / 6 gm
White pepper (*safed mirch*)
  powder — 2 tsp / 4 gm
Garam masala (see p. 6) — 2 tsp / 4 gm
Dry fenugreek (*kasoori methi*)
  powder — 1 tsp / 2 gm
Vinegar (*sirka*) — 4 tsp / 20 ml
Green coriander (*hara dhaniya*),
  chopped — 2 cups / 50 gm
Green cardamom (*choti elaichi*)
  powder — 2 tsp / 4 gm

Refined oil — 4 tbsp / 60 ml
Gram flour (*besan*) — 3 cups / 300 gm
Eggs, whisked — 4
Cream — 1 cup / 200 ml
Butter for basting

M e t h o d :

1. Wash and clean the chicken drumsticks. Remove the thigh bone from the flesh. Do not remove it completely.
2. **For the marinade,** mix all the ingredients together and rub into the chicken. Marinate for 20 minutes.
3. Heat the oil in a pan; add gram flour and stir-fry on low heat till a pleasing smell emanates. Remove from heat and transfer to a mixing bowl to cool.

4. Add 1 egg and blend to make a smooth paste; add cream and mix well.
5. Add the remaining eggs to the mixture and mix thoroughly. Coat the chicken drumsticks with this marinade and keep aside for 20 minutes.
6. Skewer the drumsticks once along the bone and once through the thigh flesh.

Cook in a tandoor for about 8-10 minutes or till slightly coloured. Remove and let excess marinade drip off.
7. Baste lightly with butter and roast again for 2-3 minutes or till completely done.
8. Remove from skewers onto a serving platter. Serve hot garnished with lemon wedges, cucumber and tomato dices, and onion rings.

Chicken

Murg Kandhari
Barbecued chicken

Preparation time: 4-5 hrs.
Cooking time: 15 min.
Serves: 4-5

Ingredients:

Chicken broiler, without skin	2 (600 gm each)
Red chilli powder	2½ tsp / 5 gm
Lemon (*nimbu*) juice	3 tbsp / 45 ml
Pomegranate (*anar*) juice	3 tbsp / 45 ml
Yoghurt (*dahi*), hung, whisked	1½ cups / 300 gm
Ginger (*adrak*) paste	2 tbsp / 36 gm
Garlic (*lasan*) paste	2 tbsp / 36 gm
Black cumin (*shah jeera*) seeds	2 tsp / 3 gm
Black pepper (*kali mirch*) powder	1 tsp / 2 gm
Garam masala (see p. 6)	2 tsp / 4 gm
Salt to taste	
Saffron (*kesar*)	1 gm
Double cream	4 tbsp / 80 ml
Butter for basting	

Method:

1. Make 3 deep incisions each on sides of breasts and thighs and 2 on each drumsticks.
2. Mix red chilli powder, lemon juice, and pomegranate juice together; rub over the chicken evenly. Marinate for 2 hours and refrigerate.
3. Mix yoghurt with remaining ingredients (except butter). Marinate chicken in this mixture for 2-3 hours more. Refrigerate.
4. Preheat the oven / tandoor / grill to 180°C / 350°F. Skewer chicken from tail to head, leaving a gap of at last 4 cm. Roast for 10 minutes. Remove, hang the skewers to let the excess moisture drip. Baste with butter and roast again for 4-5 minutes. Serve.

Murg Chakori

Chicken breasts stuffed with minced lamb

Preparation time: 40 min.
Cooking time: 30 min.
Serves: 4

Ingredients:

Chicken, breasts	8
Lamb, minced	250 gm
Black cumin (*shah jeera*) seeds	1 tsp / 2 gm
Dry ginger (*sonth*) powder	1 tsp / 2 gm
Fennel (*moti saunf*) powder	2 tsp / 4 gm
Cumin (*jeera*) powder	1 tsp / 2 gm
Red chilli powder	1 tsp / 2 gm
Coriander (*dhaniya*) powder	1 tsp / 1½ gm
Salt	2 tsp / 8 gm
Yoghurt (*dahi*)	¼ cup / 50 gm
Asafoetida (*hing*)	a pinch
Refined oil	1 cup / 200 ml
Water	1 cup / 200 ml
For the marinade:	
Yoghurt (*dahi*), drained	2½ cups / 500 gm
Salt to taste	
Cream	½ cup / 100 ml
Red chilli powder	1 tsp / 2 gm
Vinegar (*sirka*)	1½ tsp / 8 ml
Coriander powder	1 tsp / 1½ gm

Method:

1. Clean the chicken breasts, slit open from one side and flatten. Keep aside.
2. Blend together the lamb mince, black cumin seeds, dry ginger powder, fennel powder, cumin powder, red chilli powder, coriander powder, salt, yoghurt, and asafoetida.
3. Divide the mince mixture equally into balls. In a pan, heat the oil and water in equal quantities,

reduce heat and immerse the balls into the pan. Cover and cook for about 20 minutes.

4. Stuff the prepared meat balls into the chicken breasts. Wrap the chicken breasts firmly with silver foil. Poach for 15 minutes.

5. Remove from heat and unwrap the chicken breast from the foil and allow to cool.

6. **For the marinade,** blend yoghurt, salt, cream, red chilli powder, vinegar, and coriander powder. Keep aside.

7. Marinate the chicken breasts with the prepared marinade and keep aside for 15 minutes.

8. Skewer the chicken breasts and cook in a tandoor for 5-10 minutes or until golden yellow.

9. Remove from the skewers and serve hot, accompanied by tandoori roti (see p. 82).

Bharwan Tangri
Stuffed tandoori drumsticks

Preparation time: I hr.
Cooking time: I5 min.
Serves: 4

Chicken

Ingredients:

Chicken drumsticks	8
White pepper (*safed mirch*) powder	1 tsp / 2 gm
Salt to taste	
Ginger (*adrak*) paste	1 tsp / 6 gm
Garlic (*lasan*) paste	1 tsp / 6 gm

For the filling:

Cottage cheese (*paneer*), mashed	150 gm
Green chillies, finely chopped	4
Green coriander (*hara dhaniya*), finely chopped	1 tbsp / 4 gm
Cumin (*jeera*) powder	1 tsp / 1½ gm
Yellow chilli powder	½ tsp / 1 gm
Cashew nuts (*kaju*), finely chopped	1 tbsp / 10 gm
Salt to taste	

For the coating:

Cream	2 tbsp / 40 ml
Cheese, grated	1 tbsp / 15 gm
Cornflour	1 tbsp / 10 gm

Butter for basting

Method:

1. Clean the drumsticks. Make an incision along the lower half of the drumsticks, taking care not to cut through the other side. Carefully open the flap for the filling.
2. Mix white pepper, salt, ginger and garlic pastes; rub evenly over the drumsticks. Marinate for 30 minutes.

3. **For the filling,** mix cottage cheese, green chillies, green coriander, cumin powder, yellow chilli powder, cashew nuts, and salt together.

4. Put some filling into the flap of the marinated drumstick. Secure with a toothpick. Similarly, prepare the other drumsticks and refrigerate for 15 minutes.

5. **For the coating,** whisk the cream, cheese, and cornflour into a smooth paste. Coat each drumstick evenly with this paste.

6. Preheat oven / tandoor / grill to 180°C / 350°F. Skewer the drumsticks and roast for 8-10 minutes, basting occasionally with butter.

7. Remove skewers and hang for 3-4 minutes to let the excess marinade drip off.

8. Roast again for 3-4 minutes till golden. Serve hot, with mint chutney (see p. 7) and salad.

Tandoori Murg
Tandoori chicken

Preparation time: 3½ hrs.
Cooking time: 15-20 min.
Serves: 4-5

Ingredients:

Chicken, whole, skinned	2 (600 gm each)
Salt to taste	
Red chilli powder	1 tsp / 2 gm
Lemon (*nimbu*) juice	3 tbsp / 45 ml
Yoghurt (*dahi*)	½ cup / 100 gm
Cream	½ cup / 100 ml
Ginger-garlic (*adrak-lasan*) paste	2 tbsp / 36 gm
Cumin (*jeera*) powder	1 tsp / 1½ gm
Garam masala (see p. 6)	1 tsp / 2 gm
Saffron (*kesar*)	a pinch
Orange colour	a drop
Refined oil / Butter for basting	
Chaat masala	1 tsp / 2 gm

(See picture on cover)

Method:

1. Clean the chicken and make deep incisions on the breasts, thighs, and legs.

2. Mix salt, red chilli powder, and lemon juice together. Rub this paste into the chicken evenly. Keep aside for half an hour.

3. Whisk yoghurt, cream, and remaining ingredients (except last two) to make a smooth paste. Coat the chicken with this mixture. Marinate for 2½-3 hours.

4. Skewer the chicken leaving a gap of 3-4". Roast in a moderately hot tandoor / grill / oven for 8-10 minutes. Remove, baste with butter / oil and roast for another 3-4 minutes. Cut into pieces, sprinkle *chaat* masala and serve hot.

Kastoori Kebab

Chicken kebab flavoured with fenugreek

Preparation time: 1 hr.
Cooking time: 15 min.
Serves: 4-5

Chicken

I n g r e d i e n t s :

Chicken breasts, cleaned, skinned, deboned,
cut each into 2 pieces   12

For the marinade:

Ginger (*adrak*) paste	3 tbsp / 54 gm
Garlic (*lasan*) paste	3 tbsp / 54 gm
Dry fenugreek leaves (*kasoori methi*)	2 tbsp / 10 gm
White pepper (*safed mirch*) powder	1 tsp / 2 gm
Salt to taste	
Lemon (*nimbu*) juice	3 tbsp / 45 ml
Butter	4 tbsp / 80 gm
Refined oil	2 tsp / 10 ml

Gram flour (*besan*)	1 tbsp / 10 gm
Breadcrumbs	1½ tbsp / 22 gm
Ginger, chopped	3 tsp / 18 gm
Green coriander (*hara dhaniya*), chopped	1 cup / 25 gm
Black cumin (*shah jeera*) seeds	1 tsp / 2 gm
Saffron (*kesar*)	½ gm
Egg yolks	3
Green cardamom (*choti elaichi*) powder	1 tsp / 2 gm
Lemon (*nimbu*) juice to taste	

M e t h o d :

1. **For the marinade,** mix all the ingredients and rub into the chicken. Marinate for at least 1 hour.

2. Heat the butter and oil in a pan; add gram flour and stir over medium heat until golden brown. Divide this into two portions.

3. To one portion add breadcrumbs, ginger, green coriander, and marinated chicken. Mix well.

4. Preheat oven to 150°C / 300°F. To the second portion add black cumin seeds, saffron, and egg yolks; whisk the batter thoroughly.

5. Skewer 6 chicken pieces together so that they overlap. Leave a gap of 4 cm and then skewer the next lot. Coat each with the gram flour batter.

6. Roast the chicken in the oven / tandoor for 8-10 minutes. Remove and sprinkle with green cardamom powder and lemon juice.

7. Serve hot.

Shola Kebab
Spicy and aromatic lamb chunks

Preparation time: 2 hrs.
Cooking time: 15-20 min.
Serves: 4

Ingredients:

Lamb, cut into boneless pieces	900 gm
Salt	4 tsp / 16 gm
Red chilli powder	4 tsp / 8 gm
White pepper (*safed mirch*) powder	a pinch
Fenugreek (*methi*) powder	a pinch
Green cardamom (*choti elaichi*) powder	a pinch
Garam masala (see p. 6)	2 tsp / 4 gm
Onion (*kalonji*) seeds, crushed	2 tsp / 3 gm
Fennel (*moti saunf*), crushed	a pinch
Mustard seeds (*rai*), crushed	a pinch
Cumin (*jeera*) seeds, crushed	a pinch
Coriander (*dhaniya*) seeds, crushed	a pinch
Ginger-garlic (*adrak-lasan*) paste	2 tbsp / 36 gm
Raw papaya, grated	60 gm
Mustard oil	½ cup / 100 ml
Vinegar (*sirka*)	4 tsp / 20 ml
Yoghurt (*dahi*)	½ cup / 100 gm
Butter for basting	4 tsp / 20 gm

Method:

1. Prepare the marinade by mixing all the ingredients (except butter) together.
2. Rub the mixture into the lamb pieces and keep aside for 1½ hours.
3. Skewer the lamb pieces and roast in a medium hot tandoor for 10-12 minutes. Baste with butter and roast again for 5 minutes.
4. Remove from skewers and serve hot.

Lamb

Sakhat Kebab
Lamb kebab stuffed with cheese

Preparation time: 40 min.
Cooking time: 20-25 min.
Serves: 4

Ingredients:

Lamb, minced	900 gm
Salt	1 tsp / 4 gm
White pepper (*safed mirch*) powder	a pinch
Red chilli powder	½ tsp / 1 gm
Fenugreek (*methi*) powder	a pinch
Ginger-garlic (*adrak-lasan*) paste	2 tbsp / 36 gm
Green chillies, chopped	1½ tsp
Green coriander (*hara dhaniya*), chopped	1 tbsp / 4 gm
For the filling:	
Processed cheese, grated	130 gm
Green chillies, chopped	4 tsp
For the batter:	
Cornflour	7 tbsp / 70 gm
Refined flour (*maida*)	7 tbsp / 70 gm
Egg, whisked	1
Vinegar (*sirka*)	1 tsp / 5 ml
Salt to taste	
White pepper powder	a pinch
Ginger-garlic paste	1½ tsp / 9 gm
Water	1½ cups / 300 ml
Refined oil for frying	

Method:

1. Mix the lamb mince with salt, white pepper powder, red chilli powder, fenugreek powder, ginger-garlic paste, green chillies, and green coriander. Refrigerate for 15 minutes.
2. Mix green chillies and cheese together. Divide into 16 equal portions.

Lamb

36

3. **For the batter,** mix cornflour with flour, egg, vinegar, salt, white pepper powder, ginger-garlic paste, and water.

4. Make 10 cm long kebabs with the mince mixture and skewer in 4 equal parts. Roast in a tandoor for 5 minutes and remove. Allow to cool, remove from skewers in 4 pieces each.

5. Slit each kebab lengthwise and stuff the cheese mixture.

6. Dip the stuffed kebabs in the prepared batter and deep-fry in hot oil until crisp and golden brown. Remove and drain excess oil on paper towels.

7. Serve hot with mint chutney (see p. 7).

(See picture on page 2)

Kallan Kebab

Skewered rolls of lamb liver and kidney covered with chicken mince

Preparation time: I hr.
Cooking time: 20-25 min.
Serves: 4

Ingredients:

Lamb, minced	250 gm
Lamb kidney, finely chopped	125 gm
Lamb liver, finely chopped	125 gm
Salt	½ tsp / 2 gm
Red chilli powder	2 tsp / 4 gm
Garam masala (see p. 6)	1 tsp / 2 gm
Fenugreek (*methi*) powder	a pinch
Ginger-garlic (*adrak-lasan*) paste	2 tsp / 12 gm
Green coriander (*hara dhaniya*), chopped	1 tbsp / 4 gm
Green chillies, chopped	1 tsp
Chicken, minced	500 gm
Salt	½ tsp / 2 gm
White pepper (*safed mirch*) powder	½ tsp / 1 gm
Garam masala	a pinch
Fenugreek (*methi*) powder	a pinch
Ginger-garlic (*adrak-lasan*) paste	½ tsp / 3 gm
Green coriander (*hara dhaniya*), chopped	1 tbsp / 4 gm
Butter for basting	4 tsp / 20 gm

Method:

1. Mix the lamb mince, kidney, liver, salt, red chilli powder, garam masala, fenugreek powder, ginger-garlic paste, green coriander, and green chillies together. Keep aside.

Lamb

2. Skewer the lamb mince mixture and roast in a charcoal grill for 8-10 minutes. Remove from charcoal grill, place skewer upright to allow excess moisture to drip off. Keep aside for 3-5 minutes.

3. Meanwhile, mix chicken mince with the remaining ingredients (except butter).

4. Apply a coating of the chicken mince mixture evenly over the lamb mince kebabs and roast again for 5-6 minutes.

5. Baste with butter and remove the kebabs from skewers in 4 equal portions.

6. Serve immediately, accompanied by a green salad and mint chutney (see p. 7).

Masala Tandoori Gosht

Spicy lamb steaks

Preparation time: 2 hrs.
Cooking time: 7-10 min.
Serves: 4

Ingredients:

Lamb steaks (2"x 2")	8
For the marinade:	
Onion, minced	1
Garlic (*lasan*), crushed	1 tbsp / 18 gm
Green chilli paste	1 tbsp / 15 gm
Poppy seeds (*khus khus*), ground	1 tbsp / 15 gm
Garam masala (see p. 6)	1 tbsp / 5 gm
Salt to taste	

Method:

1. **For the marinade,** mix onion, garlic, green chilli paste, poppy seed paste, garam masala, and salt together. Rub into the lamb steaks. Marinate for 2 hours.

2. Roast in a charcoal grill / tandoor till cooked as desired.

3. Serve hot, garnished with onion rings and accompanied by pickled green chillies.

Peshawari Kebab

Succulent lamb coated with papaya and yoghurt

Preparation time: 1¼ hrs.
Cooking time: 30 min.
Serves: 4

I n g r e d i e n t s :

Lamb, boneless, cut into 1" cubes.   1 kg
For the marinade:
Yoghurt (*dahi*)   ½ cup / 100 gm
Raw papaya paste   2 tsp / 10 gm
Salt to taste
Red chilli powder   2 tsp / 4 gm
Garam masala (see p. 6)   1 tsp / 2 gm
Black cumin (*shah jeera*) seeds   1 tsp / 2 gm
Ginger (*adrak*) paste   1 tbsp / 18 gm
Garlic (*lasan*) paste   1 tsp / 6 gm

Ghee for basting
Chaat masala   1 tsp / 2 gm
Juice of lemon (*nimbu*)   1

M e t h o d :

1. **For the marinade,** mix all the ingredients and rub well into the lamb. Leave aside for an hour.
2. Skewer the meat pieces and cook in a tandoor till half done.
3. Remove and leave to cool for 10 minutes.
4. Baste with ghee and cook for 8 more minutes.
5. Sprinkle with *chaat* masala and lemon juice. Serve hot with a green salad.

Lamb

Seekh Kebab

Spicy minced meat skewered and roasted

Preparation time: 45 min.
Cooking time: 15 min.
Serves: 4

Ingredients:

Lamb, minced	500 gm
Black cardamoms (*badi elaichi*)	2
Black peppercorns (*sabut kali mirch*)	2 tsp
Cinnamon (*dalchini*) powder	½ tsp / 1 gm
Cloves (*laung*)	2
Coconut (*nariyal*), grated	1 tbsp / 4 gm
Cream	2 tbsp / 40 ml
Cumin (*jeera*) seeds	1 tsp / 2 gm
Garlic (*lasan*) paste	3 tsp / 18 gm
Ginger (*adrak*) paste	3 tsp / 18 gm
Gram flour (*besan*), roasted	3 tbsp / 30 gm
Mace (*javitri*) powder	½ tsp / 1 gm
Refined oil	1 tbsp / 15 ml
Onion paste, browned	2 tbsp / 50 gm
Poppy seeds (*khus khus*)	2 tsp / 4 gm
Raw papaya paste	1 tbsp / 15 gm
Red chilli powder	1 tsp / 2 gm
Yoghurt (*dahi*)	2 tbsp / 60 gm

Method:

1. Mix mince with all the other ingredients. Knead well for 10 minutes. Let it stand for 10 minutes.
2. Moisten hands with water and mould the mixture around skewers pressing and shaping to about 5½″ long kebabs. Roast in a moderately hot tandoor for 12 minutes till they are browned uniformly.
3. The kebabs can also be slid off the skewers and cooked on fine wire mesh of the grilling rack in a charcoal gas grill. Do not turn too often as they may split. Serve hot with mint chutney (see p. 7).

Lamb

Barah Kebab
Skewered and roasted lamb chops

Preparation time: 4½ hrs.
Cooking time: 1 hr.
Serves: 4

L a m b

Ingredients:

Lamb, chops and leg pieces	900 gm
For the marinade:	
Salt to taste	
Red chilli powder	2 tsp / 4 gm
Garam masala (see p. 6)	4 tsp / 8 gm
Malt vinegar (*sirka*)	¾ cup / 150 ml
Ginger (*adrak*) paste	3 tbsp / 54 gm
Garlic (*lasan*) paste	3 tbsp / 54 gm
Raw papaya paste	4 tsp / 20 gm
or *Kachri* (tenderizer)	4 tsp / 20 gm
Black cumin (*shah jeera*) seeds	3 tbsp / 18 gm
Yoghurt (*dahi*)	¼ cup / 50 gm

Refined oil for basting

Method:

1. **For the marinade,** mix all the ingredients together and rub into the lamb. Keep aside for 4 hours or overnight.
2. Skewer the pieces 1″ apart and roast on a slow fire in a tandoor or charcoal grill for 15 minutes or till half done.
3. Stand at room temperature for 20 minutes. Baste with oil.
4. Roast or grill on slow fire for another 20 minutes till velvety brown.
5. Serve with onion rings and lemon wedges.

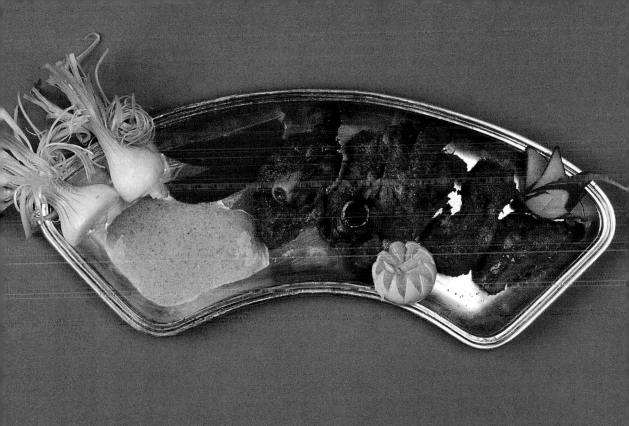

Pasinda Kebab
Thin meat slices roasted on skewers

Preparation time: 3½ hrs.
Cooking time: 15 min.
Serves: 4

I n g r e d i e n t s :

Lean meat slab	450 gm
Blend together:	
Cloves (*laung*)	5
Green cardamoms (*choti elaichi*)	5
Raw papaya paste	1½ tsp / 7½ gm
Or *Kachri* (tenderizer)	1 tsp / 5 gm
Garlic (*lasan*), chopped	10 cloves
Onions, chopped	¼ cup / 30 gm
Ginger (*adrak*), chopped	2″ piece / 15 gm
Cumin (*jeera*) seeds	1 tsp / 2 gm
Coconut (*nariyal*), desiccated	2 tbsp / 8 gm
Nutmeg (*jaiphal*) powder	¼ tsp
Black peppercorns (*sabut kali mirch*)	16
Poppy seeds (*khus khus*)	1 tsp / 2 gm
Yoghurt (*dahi*)	¾ cup / 150 gm
Red chilli powder	1 tsp / 2 gm
Salt to taste	

Butter for basting

M e t h o d :

1. Cut meat into slices 3½″ long, 1¼″ wide and ¾″ thick. Cut the slice into half without cutting through, leaving a join at the end. Open the cut halves to make a single strip, approximately 6″ long. Beat the joints with the back of a knife to flatten them a bit.
2. Blend all the ingredients together to a fine paste.
3. Coat the strips with this mixture and leave to marinate for 3 hours.

4. Weave the skewer in and out of the meat strips at 4 points, at regular intervals. The meat will resemble a wavy line, with the skewer running through its centre.

5. Roast over an open charcoal fire or barbeque for 10 minutes. When one side is cooked, baste with butter and roast again for 3-5 minutes.

6. Serve as a salad with sliced onions, green chillies, and finely chopped mint leaves.

No tears, no fears!

To prevent your eyes from watering when cutting onions, dip the knife in hot water.

Khatta Pudina Chops

Tangy mint lamb chops

Preparation time: 4 hrs.
Cooking time: 12-15 minutes
Serves: 4-5

Ingredients:

Lamb chops, cleaned	1 kg
Cumin (*jeera*) powder	1 tsp / 1½ gm
White pepper (*safed mirch*)	1 tbsp / 5 gm
Garam masala (see p. 6)	2 tsp / 4 gm
Lemon (*nimbu*) juice	5 tsp / 25 ml
Salt to taste	
Cream	4 tbsp / 80 ml
Yoghurt (*dahi*), drained	¾ cup / 150 gm
Mint chutney (see p. 6)	1¼ cup / 250 gm
Cornflour	2 tbsp / 20 gm
Papaya paste (optional)	3 tbsp / 45 gm
Garlic (*lasan*) paste	1 tbsp / 18 gm
Ginger (*adrak*) paste	1 tbsp / 18 gm
Fenugreek (*methi*) powder	1 tsp / 2 gm
Refined oil for basting	

Method:

1. Mix cumin powder, white pepper, garam masala, lemon juice, and salt together. Rub the paste into the lamb chops and marinate for 1 hour.

2. Mix cream, yoghurt, mint chutney, and cornflour. Add the remaining ingredients (except oil) and whisk to a fine paste. Mix with lamb chops and marinate for another 2½-3 hours.

3. Skewer lamb chops 2 cm apart and roast in a preheated (180°C / 350°F) oven / tandoor / charcoal grill for 8-10 minutes. Hang the skewers for a few minutes to allow excess marinade to drip off. Baste with oil and roast for another 4-5 minutes.

4. Sprinkle lemon juice, garnish with slices of cucumber, tomato, and onion; serve hot.

Lamb

Raan

Roast leg of lamb flavoured with yoghurt

Preparation time: 2½ hrs.
Cooking time: 2 hrs.
Serves: 4

Ingredients:

Lamb, leg piece   1

For the marinade:

Brown onion paste (see p. 7)   4 tbsp / 100 gm
Garlic (*lasan*) paste   2 tsp / 12 gm
Ginger (*adrak*) paste   2 tsp / 12 gm
Green cardamom (*choti elaichi*) powder   ½ tsp
Yoghurt (*dahi*)   4 tbsp / 120 gm
Red chilli powder   2 tsp / 4 gm
Salt to taste
Garam masala (see p. 6)   ½ tsp
Black pepper (*kali mirch*) powder   1 tsp / 2 gm
Saffron (*kesar*)   a pinch

Refined oil for basting
Chaat masala to taste

Method:

1. Clean the leg of lamb and prick thoroughly down to the bone with a fork. Mix all the ingredients of the marinade together. Apply evenly on the lamb and leave to marinate for 2 hours.
2. Place leg in a baking tray with 2 cups water. Bake in a preheated (180°C / 350°F) oven for at least one hour turning the leg twice / thrice to ensure that the leg cooks evenly. Roast till the liquid dries up.
3. Baste with oil and grill / roast in a moderately hot tandoor till well done.
4. Sprinkle *chaat* masala and garnish with onion rings. Serve with mint chutney (see p. 7).

Lamb

Mahi Tikka
Fish tikka

Preparation time: 2½ hrs.
Cooking time: 15-20 min.
Serves: 4

Ingredients:

Fish, cut into boneless pieces	1 kg
Ghee	½ cup / 100 gm
Onions, sliced	½ cup / 60 gm
Garlic (*lasan*), chopped	3 tbsp / 36 gm
Salt to taste	
Red chilli powder	2 tbsp
Coriander (*dhaniya*) powder	2 tsp / 3 gm
Cumin (*jeera*) powder	1 tsp / 1½ gm
Turmeric (*haldi*) powder	1 tsp / 2 gm
Yoghurt (*dahi*)	½ cup / 100 gm

Butter for basting

Method:

1. Heat the ghee in a pan; fry the onions till brown. Remove, drain excess ghee and blend the onions to a smooth paste.
2. In the same pan, fry the garlic and keep aside.
3. Allow the ghee to cool. Mix the onion paste, garlic, the remaining ingredients, and fish pieces with the ghee and keep aside for 2 hours.
4. Skewer the fish pieces and roast in a tandoor / oven / grill for 5-10 minutes. Remove, baste with butter and cook further for 3-5 minutes.
5. Remove from skewers and serve hot.

Saloni Macchi Tikka

Fish chunks cooked in a spicy marinade

Preparation time: **40 min.**
Cooking time: **15-20 min.**
Serves: **4**

Ingredients:

Fish, cut into boneless pieces	800 gm
For the marinade:	
Salt	1 tbsp
White pepper (*safed mirch*) powder	1 tsp / 2 gm
Fenugreek (*methi*) powder	½ tsp
Turmeric (*haldi*) powder	½ tsp
Red chilli powder	1½ tsp / 3 gm
Garam masala (see p. 6)	1 tsp / 2 gm
Clove (*laung*) powder	a pinch
Ginger-garlic (*adrak-lasan*) paste	5 tsp / 30 gm
Yoghurt (*dahi*), drained	2 tsp / 10 gm
Vinegar (*sirka*)	¾ cup / 150 ml
Cream	½ cup / 100 gm
Mustard oil	4 tbsp / 60 ml
Cloves (*laung*)	16
Charcoal piece, live	1
Refined oil for basting	

Method:

1. Wash, clean and dry the fish pieces.
2. **For the marinade,** mix all the ingredients together and rub into the fish pieces and keep aside.
3. Make a well in the centre and put mustard oil and cloves. Place the live charcoal piece in the oil and cover the bowl with a lid. Seal the lid so that the smoke does not escape. Keep aside for 30 minutes.
4. Remove the lid, skewer the fish and roast in a

medium hot tandoor for 5-6 minutes. Remove from the tandoor and allow excess marinade to drip off.

5. Baste with oil and roast again for 2 minutes until done. Remove from skewers and transfer to a serving platter.

6. Serve hot accompanied by a green salad and mint chutney (see p. 7).

Lime & Lemony!

To remove the odour of fish or garlic from hands, wash with salt or lemon and cold water before using soap.

Bharwan Tandoori Macchi

Stuffed tandoori fish

Preparation time: 3½ hrs.
Cooking time: 20 min.
Serves: 4-5

Ingredients:

River or sea fish
  (with single centre bone)   5 (400 gm each)
Salt to taste
Malt vinegar (*sirka*)   3 tbsp / 45 ml
Yoghurt (*dahi*), drained   1 cup / 200 gm
Black pepper (*kali mirch*) powder   2 tsp / 4 gm
Fennel (*moti saunf*)   2 tsp / 4 gm
Garlic (*lasan*) paste   5 tsp / 30 gm
Ghee   3 tbsp / 45 gm
Ginger (*adrak*) paste   5 tsp / 30 gm
Gram flour (*besan*)   4 tbsp / 40 gm
Lemon (*nimbu*) juice   5 tsp / 25 ml
Red chilli powder   4 tsp / 8 gm
Turmeric (*haldi*) powder   2 tsp / 4 gm
Butter to baste   2½ tbsp / 50 gm

Method:

1. Marinate fish in vinegar and salt.
2. In a bowl, mix yoghurt with the remaining ingredients (except butter) and make a fine paste.
3. Marinate the fish in this paste and leave to stand for 2-3 hours.
4. Preheat the oven to 180°C / 350°F.
5. Skewer the fish from mouth to tail, 4 cm apart. Roast in the oven for 12-15 minutes.
6. Baste with butter. Remove and hang the skewers to let excess marinade drip off.
7. Serve hot, garnished with slices of cucumber, tomato and onion rings; accompanied by mint chutney (see p. 7).

Jhinga Mehrunisa

Tandoori prawns in a rich and creamy marinade

Preparation time: 40 min.
Cooking time: 10 min.
Serves: 4

Ingredients:

Prawns, shelled, deveined	1.4 kg
Vinegar (*sirka*)	3 tbsp / 45 ml
Salt to taste	
For the marinade:	
Lemon (*nimbu*) juice	4 tsp / 20 ml
Yoghurt (*dahi*)	1¼ cups / 250 gm
Cream	1 cup / 200 ml
White pepper (*safed mirch*) powder	1½ tsp / 3 gm
Cheese, grated	80 gm
Dry fenugreek (*kasoori methi*) powder	2 tsp / 4 gm
Ginger-garlic (*adrak-lasan*) paste	2 tbsp / 36 gm
Garam masala (see p. 6)	1½ tsp / 3 gm
Saffron (*kesar*)	a few strands
Butter for basting	

Method:

1. Wash the prawns with vinegar and salt water. Drain and pat dry.
2. **For the marinade,** mix all the ingredients together. Rub into the prawns and marinate for 30 minutes.
3. Skewer the prawns and roast in a moderately hot tandoor for 6-8 minutes. Remove from tandoor and allow excess marinade to drip off.
4. Baste lightly with butter and roast again for 2-3 minutes. Remove from skewers and serve with mint chutney (see p. 7)

Jalpari Kebab
Saffron flavoured fish rolls stuffed with prawns

Preparation time: 40 min.
Cooking time: 20 min.
Serves: 4

Ingredients:

Fish fillets, thin	12
Prawns, shelled, deveined	220 gm
Ginger-garlic (*adrak-lasan*) paste	5 tsp / 30 gm
Mango pickle masala	5 tsp / 25 gm
Carom (*ajwain*) seeds	1 tsp / 2 gm
White pepper (*safed mirch*) powder	1 tsp / 2 gm
Garam masala (see p. 6)	2 tsp / 4 gm
Salt to taste	
Red chilli powder	1 tsp / 2 gm
Lemon (*nimbu*) juice	1 tsp / 5 ml
Refined oil	4 tsp / 20 ml
Yoghurt (*dahi*), drained	¾ cup / 150 gm
Cream	2 tbsp / 40 ml
Saffron (*kesar*)	a few strands
Green cardamom (*choti elaichi*) powder	a pinch
Water	5 cups / 1 lt

Method:

1. Extract juice from ginger-garlic paste and keep aside.
2. Clean the fish fillets and prawns. Pat dry with a cloth.
3. Make a marinade with ginger-garlic juice, mango pickle masala, half of carom seeds, white pepper powder, garam masala, salt, red chilli powder, lemon juice, and oil.
4. Marinate the fish fillets in the prepared marinade and keep aside for 5 minutes.

5. Prepare second marinade of yoghurt, cream, saffron, green cardamom powder, and remaining half of other ingredients. Keep aside.
6. Put one fish fillet flat on a tabletop. Place a prawn at one end of the fillet and roll the fillet. Wrap it tightly with cling wrap or aluminium foil.
7. Boil water in a pot and cook the rolls for 10 minutes keeping the pot covered.
8. Drain the water and place the rolls under running water for 1 minute. Remove the foil.
9. Marinate the rolls in the second marinade for 5 minutes.
10. Skewer the rolls and roast in hot tandoor or in an oven (150-180°C / 300°-350°F) for 10 minutes.
11. Remove from skewers, transfer to a serving platter and serve hot with mint chutney (see p. 7).

(See picture on page 4)

Tandoori Jhinga

Tandoori prawns

Preparation time: 2 hrs.
Cooking time: 15 min.
Serves: 4

Ingredients:

Prawns, king size	12
Ginger (*adrak*) paste	1½ tsp / 9 gm
Garlic (*lasan*) paste	2 tsp / 12 gm
Lemon (*nimbu*) juice	2 tbsp / 30 ml
Yoghurt (*dahi*)	1 cup / 200 gm
Gram flour (*besan*)	2 tbsp / 20 gm
Salt to taste	
Carom (*ajwain*) seeds	1 tsp / 2 gm
Red chilli powder	1 tsp / 2 gm
Garam masala (see p. 6)	1 tsp / 2 gm
Turmeric (*haldi*) powder	½ tsp / 1 gm
Refined oil for basting	
Chaat masala to taste	

Method:

1. Mix ginger-garlic pastes and 1 tbsp lemon juice together; rub into the prawns and keep aside.
2. Whisk together yoghurt, gram flour, salt, carom seeds, red chilli powder, garam masala, and turmeric powder into a smooth paste. Marinate the prawns in the paste for at least 2 hours.
3. Skewer the prawns gently and cook in a preheated (150°C / 300°F) oven / tandoor / grill / for about 12-15 minutes or till almost done.
4. Hang skewers for 3-5 minutes to allow excess marinade to drip off. Baste with oil and roast again for 3-5 minutes or till golden brown. Remove.
5. Sprinkle *chaat* masala and remaining lemon juice. Serve hot with a salad of your choice.

Jhinga Nisha
Prawns flavoured with sesame seeds and fenugreek

Preparation time: 1½ hrs.
Cooking time: 20 min.
Serves: 4

Ingredients:

Prawns	8
Lemon (*nimbu*) juice	1 tsp / 5 ml
Ginger-garlic (*adrak-lasan*) paste	4 tsp / 24 gm
Salt to taste	
Sesame (*til*) seeds	3 tsp / 9 gm
Yoghurt (*dahi*)	4 tsp / 20 gm
Cheddar cheese	3 tsp / 15 gm
Cinnamon (*dalchini*) powder	1 tsp / 2 gm
Dry fenugreek (*kasoori methi*) leaves	1 tsp
White pepper (*safed mirch*) powder	1 tsp / 2 gm
Green chillies	6
Clove (*laung*) powder	1 tsp / 2 gm
Chaat masala	1 tsp / 2 gm

Method:

1. Rub lemon juice, ginger-garlic paste, and salt on the prawns and keep aside for half an hour.
2. Roast the sesame seeds and crush to a powder.
3. Beat the yoghurt in a bowl and add the remaining ingredients (except *chaat* masala).
4. Rub this mixture on the prawns and keep in a cool place for 1 hour. Preheat the oven to 150°C / 300°F.
5. Skewer the prawns and roast till light golden in colour. Apply the sesame seed powder over the prawns and roast again for 2 minutes. Sprinkle with *chaat* masala and lemon juice.

Tandoori Lobster

Preparation time: 4½ hrs.
Cooking time: 10 min.
Serves: 4-5

Ingredients:

Lobsters, medium-sized, halved	4
Ginger (*adrak*) paste	4 tsp / 24 gm
Garlic (*lasun*) paste	4 tsp / 24 gm
Carom (*ajwain*) seeds	½ tsp
Malt vinegar (*sirka*)	½ cup / 100 ml
Salt to taste	
Yoghurt (*dahi*), drained	1 cup / 200 gm
White pepper (*safed mirch*) powder	1 tsp / 2 gm
Garam masala (see p. 6)	2 tsp / 4 gm
Egg	1
Cottage cheese (*paneer*)	60 gm
Gram flour (*besan*)	3 tbsp / 30 gm
Mustard oil	4 tbsp / 60 ml
Red chilli paste	1 tsp / 5 gm

Method:

1. Shell and devein the lobsters. Wash and dry the shells and dip them in hot oil. Drain. Keep aside.
2. Marinate lobsters in ginger and garlic pastes, carom seeds, vinegar, and salt for 1 hour.
3. Whisk yoghurt in a large bowl. Add the remaining ingredients; coat the lobsters with this mixture; keep aside for 3 hours.
4. Skewer the lobsters 2 cm apart. Keep a tray underneath to collect the excess drippings. Roast in a medium-hot tandoor / oven for 5 minutes.
5. Baste with butter and roast again for 2 minutes.
6. Place the lobster in the shell; garnish with lettuce, tomato slices, and onion rings. Serve hot.

Baida Kebab

Skewered egg and potato rolls

Preparation time: 30-40 min.
Cooking time: 10-15 min.
Serves: 4

Vegetarian

Ingredients:

Eggs	11
Potatoes, boiled, mashed	200 gm
Garam masala (see p. 6)	1 tsp / 2 gm
Chaat masala	1 tsp / 2 gm
Breadcrumbs	½ cup / 60 gm
Salt	1½ tsp / 6 gm
Red chilli powder	1 tsp / 2 gm
Ginger (*adrak*), chopped	2 tsp / 12 gm
Green chillies, chopped	1 tsp
Green coriander (*hara dhaniya*), chopped	1 tbsp / 4 gm
Butter for basting	2 tbsp / 40 gm

Method:

1. Boil 10 eggs, grate and keep aside.
2. Mix together the grated eggs, mashed potatoes, garam masala, *chaat* masala, breadcrumbs, salt, red chilli powder, ginger, green chillies, green coriander, and the raw egg.
3. Divide this mixture into 5 equal portions
4. Wrap each portion along the length of skewers using wet hands leaving a 2 cm gap between each. Roast for 5-10 minutes.
5. Remove and baste with butter. Roast further for 3-5 minutes or until cooked.
6. Remove from skewers and serve hot with mint chutney (see p. 7).

Paneer Seekh Kebab

Skewered cottage cheese kebab

Preparation time: 15 min.
Cooking time: 15 min.
Serves: 4-5

Vegetarian

Ingredients:

Cottage cheese (*paneer*), grated	1 kg
Green chillies, chopped	30 gm
Onions, grated	2
Ginger (*adrak*), coarsely ground	1 tbsp / 18 gm
Green coriander (*hara dhaniya*), chopped	2 tbsp / 8 gm
Black pepper (*kali mirch*)	2 tsp / 4 gm
Cumin (*jeera*) powder	1 tsp / 2 gm
Red chilli powder	1 tsp / 2 gm
Salt to taste	
Cornflour	2 tbsp / 20 gm
Butter for basting	

Method:

1. Mix all the ingredients, adding the cornflour in the end and knead well.
2. Moisten hands and wrap the cottage cheese mixture around the skewers to form a kebab 4-5" long and 2" apart.
3. Roast in a preheated (150°C / 300°F) oven / tandoor / charcoal grill for 5-6 minutes, basting occasionally with melted butter.
4. Serve hot with salad and mint chutney (see p.7).

Bharwan Shimla Mirch

Stuffed capsicum

Preparation time: 30 min.
Cooking time: 10 min.
Serves: 4-5

Ingredients:

Capsicums (*Shimla mirch*), large	6
Butter / Refined oil	1 tbsp / 15 ml
Spring onions, chopped	120 gm
Green coriander (*hara dhaniya*), chopped	1 tbsp / 4 gm
Cottage cheese (*paneer*), grated	250 gm
Salt to taste	
Chaat masala	1 tbsp
Green chillies, chopped	4
Cumin (*jeera*) powder	2 tsp / 3 gm

Method:

1. Slice each capsicum from the top. Scoop out the seeds and keep capsicum cup and top aside.
2. Heat the butter / oil in a pan; stir-fry the spring onions. Add the remaining ingredients. Cook further for 4-5 minutes. Remove from heat.
3. Fill the cottage cheese mixture into the capsicum cups and cover the top with the capsicum slice. Secure with toothpicks.
4. Preheat oven to 150°C / 300°F. Place stuffed capsicums on a baking tray or skewer carefully and grill on charcoal for 8-10 minutes till the skin develops golden brown spots. Remove toothpicks and serve hot.

Kastoori Paneer Tikka

Cottage cheese flavoured with fenugreek

Preparation time: 2¼ hrs.
Cooking time: 10 min.
Serves: 4-5

Ingredients:

Cottage cheese (*paneer*)	1 kg
Black cumin (*shah jeera*) seeds	1 tsp / 2 gm
White pepper (*safed mirch*)	1 tsp / 2 gm
Garam masala (see p. 6)	2 tsp / 4 gm
Lemon (*nimbu*) juice	5 tsp / 25 ml
Salt to taste	
Cottage cheese (*paneer*), grated	50 gm
Cream	½ cup / 100 ml
Yoghurt (*dahi*), hung	¾ cup / 150 gm
Gram flour (*besan*) / cornflour	2 tbsp / 20 gm
Dry fenugreek (*kasoori methi*)	4 tsp / 2 gm
Chaat masala (optional)	2 tsp / 4 gm
Ginger-garlic (*adrak-lasan*) paste	2 tbsp / 36 gm
Red chilli powder	2 tsp / 4 gm
Butter to baste	

Method:

1. Wash and cut the cottage cheese into 4 cm cubes.
2. Mix black cumin seeds, white pepper, garam masala, 4 tsp lemon juice, and salt together. Mix in grated cottage cheese and refrigerate for 1 hour.
3. Whisk the remaining ingredients (except butter) to a fine batter. Add the cottage cheese cubes, mix well and marinate for at least 1 hour.
4. Preheat the oven to 150°C / 300°F. Thread the cubes 2 cm apart on a skewer. Roast in an oven / tandoor / charcoal grill for 5-6 minutes. Baste with butter.
5. Serve hot sprinkled with *chaat* masala and remaining lemon juice, accompanied with mint chutney (see p. 7)

Dum Saunfia Tikka

Cottage cheese layered with fennel

Preparation time: 2½ hrs.
Cooking time: 10 min.
Serves: 4

Vegetarian

Ingredients:

Cottage cheese (*paneer*)	900 gm
Yoghurt (*dahi*)	½ cup / 100 gm
Cream	¼ cup / 50 ml
Red chilli powder	1 tsp / 2 gm
Yellow chilli powder	1 tbsp
White pepper (*safed mirch*) powder	1 tsp / 2 gm
Carom (*ajwain*) seeds	1 tsp / 2 gm
Salt to taste	
Raisins (*kishmish*)	3 tbsp / 30 gm
Fennel (*moti saunf*), powdered	2 tsp / 4 gm
Sugar	2 tsp / 6 gm
Mint chutney (see p. 7)	½ cup / 100 gm

Method:

1. Hang the yoghurt in a muslin cloth for 2 hours, till whey is drained. Add cream, red chilli powder, yellow chilli powder, white pepper powder, carom seeds, and salt; mix well.
2. Add raisins, fennel powder, and sugar to the mint chutney.
3. Cut cottage cheese into 1½″ cubes. Slit the cubes and spread with mint chutney mixture.
4. Press halves together again.
5. Marinade the cheese cubes in the yoghurt-cream-spice mixture for 15 minutes.
6. Put on skewers and cook in a preheated oven at 140°C / 275°F for 5 minutes. Serve hot as a snack.

Tandoori Paneer Salad

Tandoori cottage cheese and vegetable salad

Preparation time: 2 hrs.
Cooking time: 15 min.
Serves: 4-5

I n g r e d i e n t s :

Cottage cheese (*paneer*)	1 kg
Capsicum (*Shimla mirch*)	20 gm
Tomato	20 gm
Onion	20 gm
Pineapple (*ananas*)	20 gm
Black cumin (*shahi jeera*) seeds	½ tsp
White pepper (*safed mirch*) powder	1 tsp / 2 gm
Garam masala (see p. 6)	2 tsp / 4 gm
Turmeric (*haldi*) powder	1 tsp / 2 gm
Lemon (*nimbu*) juice	1 tbsp / 15 ml
Salt to taste	
Cream	½ cup / 100 ml
Yoghurt (*dahi*), drained	¾ cup / 150 gm
Gram flour (*besan*) / cornflour	2 tbsp / 20 gm
Red chilli powder	2 tsp / 4 gm
Saffron (*kesar*)	½ tsp
Ginger (*adrak*) paste	1 tbsp / 18 gm
Garlic (*lasan*) paste	1 tbsp / 18 gm
Butter for basting	
Chaat masala (optional)	2 tsp / 4 gm

M e t h o d :

1. Wash and cut the cottage cheese, vegetables, and pineapple into 4 cm cubes.
2. Mix black cumin seeds, white pepper, garam masala, turmeric powder, two-thirds of the lemon juice, and salt together. Add the cottage cheese cubes to this mixture and refrigerate for 1 hour.

3. Mix together cream, yoghurt, and gram flour / cornflour. Add remaining ingredients (except butter and *chaat* masala) and whisk to a fine batter.

4. Add the refrigerated cottage cheese cubes, pineapple and vegetables cubes to the batter and leave to marinate for at least another 1 hour.

5. Preheat oven to 150-180°C / 300-350°F.

6. Skewer 6 cottage cheese cubes and 4 vegetable-pineapple pieces per skewer (one portion) and pack tightly together.

7. Roast in an oven / tandoor / charcoal grill for 5-6 minutes, basting regularly with melted butter.

8. Sprinkle *chaat* masala and the remaining lemon juice. Serve hot, garnished with slices of cucumber, tomato and onion.

Tandoori Aloo

Potatoes stuffed with lightly spiced dry fruits

Preparation time: 20 min.
Cooking time: 15 min.
Serves: 4

Vegetarian

Ingredients:

Potatoes, large	1 kg / 8
Refined oil for frying	
Salt to taste	
Red chilli powder	1 tsp / 2 gm
Garam masala (see p. 6)	a pinch
Lemon (*nimbu*) juice	1 tsp / 5 ml
Cashew nuts (*kaju*), broken	5-10
Raisins (*kishmish*)	1 tbsp / 10 gm
Ghee	2 tsp / 10 gm
Cheese, grated	20 gm
Green coriander (*hara dhaniya*), chopped	1 tbsp / 4 gm
Chaat masala	½ tsp

Method:

1. Peel the potatoes. Scoop out the centre leaving thin walls at the sides.
2. Fry the potato shells and the scoops separately. Do not let them change colour but let the sides become crisp.
3. Cool the scooped out portion of the potatoes and mash. Add salt, red chilli powder, garam masala, lemon juice, cashew nuts, raisins, and ghee.
4. Stuff the mixture into the potato cases.
5. Arrange 4 pieces on one skewer and sprinkle grated cheese on top. Grill till golden brown in colour.
6. Sprinkle with green coriander and *chaat* masala, serve hot.

Tandoori Phool

Batter fried cauliflower roasted in tandoor

Preparation time: 45 min.
Cooking time: 20 min.
Serves: 4

Vegetarian

Ingredients:

Cauliflowers (*phool gobi*),
  break into florets,
    washed, dried   800 gm / 2 small flowers
Salt to taste
Chaat masala   4 tsp / 8 gm
Juice of lemons (*nimbu*)   2
Gram flour (*besan*)   4 tbsp / 40 gm
Red chilli powder   2 tsp / 4 gm
Refined oil for frying and basting
Cucumber (*khira*), sliced   1
Tomatoes, cut into wedges   2

Method:

1. Marinate the florets in a mixture of salt, *chaat* masala, and lemon juice for 30 minutes.
2. Mix gram flour with ½ cup water into a smooth batter. Season with salt and red chilli powder.
3. Heat the oil in a frying pan; dip the florets in the batter and lower gently into the hot oil; fry over a low flame. Remove. Once the florets are cool, cut into pieces.
4. Put on skewers and roast in a tandoor for 5-6 minutes till golden brown or roast in a preheated oven at 140°C / 275°F for 10 minutes. Baste with oil while roasting. Remove from skewers and serve with cucumber and tomato wedges.

Tandoori Roti

Unleavened, wholewheat flour bread

Preparation time: 30 min.
Cooking time: 7 min. for each roti
Serves: 4

Ingredients:

Wholewheat flour (*atta*)   2 cups / 200 gm
Ghee to grease baking tray
Refined flour (*maida*) to dust
Salt to taste

Method:

1. Sieve the wholewheat flour with salt onto a kneading platter.
2. Make a well in the flour and pour approximately 1½ cups water into it. Gradually mix the flour and water and then knead to a soft dough.
3. Cover with a damp cloth and keep aside for 20 minutes.
4. Divide the dough into 8 portions. Make into balls and dust with flour.
5. Pat and flatten each ball with the palms to make 6"-wide discs.
6. Wearing an oven glove stick the disc to the side of a moderately hot tandoor. Bake for 2 minutes then peel off swiftly. Alternatively, place on a greased baking tray and bake for 5-6 minutes at 180°C / 350°F in a preheated oven.
7. Serve hot with any curry.

(*See picture **left:** tandoori roti; **right:** khameeri roti*)

Khameeri Roti
Leavened bread

Preparation time: I hr.
Cooking time: 4-5 min. for each roti
Serves: 4

I n g r e d i e n t s :

Wholewheat flour (*atta*)   2 cups / 200 gm
Salt to taste
Yeast, fresh   1½ tsp
Ghee to grease baking tray.
Refined flour (*maida*) to dust

M e t h o d :

1. Dissolve the yeast in ½ cup warm water.
2. Sieve the wholewheat flour with salt onto a platter.
3. Make a well in the flour and pour 1 cup water. Mix flour and water gradually, then knead into a tough dough. Cover with a damp cloth and keep aside for 15 minutes.
4. Slowly sprinkle the dissolved yeast over the dough and keep kneading till the dough is smooth and pliable and not sticky. Cover with a damp cloth and keep aside for 30 minutes.
5. Divide the dough into 8 equal balls and dust with dry flour.
6. Press and flatten each ball into round discs, 8″ wide. Wearing an oven glove stick the disc to the side of a hot tandoor and bake for 2 minutes. Remove with a pair of tongs. Alternatively, place on a greased baking tray and bake for 4-5 minutes in a preheated oven at 180°C / 350°F. Serve hot.

Naan
A light, leavened bread

Preparation time: 2½ hrs.
Cooking time: 15 min. for each naan
Serves: 4

Ingredients:

Refined flour (*maida*)	2 cups / 200 gm
Salt to taste	
Baking soda	¼ tsp
Baking powder	1 tsp / 6 gm
Whisk together:	
Milk	3 tbsp / 45 ml
Sugar	2 tsp / 6 gm
Yoghurt (*dahi*)	5 tsp / 25 gm
Groundnut oil	2 tbsp / 30 ml
Onion seeds (*kalonji*)	1 tsp / 2 gm
Melon (*magaz*) seeds	1 tsp / 2 gm
Ghee to grease tray	
White butter	2 tbsp / 40 gm

Method:

1. Sieve first 4 ingredients onto a kneading platter. Make a well in the centre; mix in 1 cup water and milk mixture and knead to make a dough. Cover with a moist cloth and keep aside for 10 minutes.

2. Add oil and knead again. Cover the dough and keep aside for 2 hours till it rises. Divide the dough into 6 balls. Flatten balls and sprinkle onion and melon seeds. Cover and keep aside for 5 minutes.

3. Roll and flatten each ball between your palms. Stretch dough to one side to give an elongated shape. Using oven gloves, stick the naan inside a hot tandoor for 3 minutes or place the naan on a greased tray and bake in an oven for 10 minutes at 180°C / 350°F. Apply butter (optional) and serve.

Taftan
Rich, leavened, rice flour bread

Preparation time: 1 hr.
Cooking time: 10 min. for each *taftan*
Serves: 4

Accompaniments

Ingredients:

Rice flour	2 cups / 200 gm
Salt to taste	
Water	½ cup / 100 ml
Sugar	½ tsp
Milk	1 cup / 200 ml
Ghee	¾ cup / 150 gm
Yeast	½ tsp
Melon (*magaz*) seeds	2 tsp / 4 gm
Green coriander (*hara dhaniya*), chopped	1 tbsp / 4 gm
Butter or ghee for brushing	

Method:

1. Sieve flour and salt together.
2. Make a well in the flour and add water, sugar, milk, ghee, yeast, and melon seeds. Mix gradually and knead into a soft dough.
3. Divide into 4 equal balls and keep aside for half an hour.
4. Dust lightly and roll into 3½" discs, ¼" thick. Sprinkle with green coriander.
5. Put into a tandoor and bake till brown.
6. Brush with ghee.
7. Serve hot.

(*See picture* **left:** taftan; **right:** naan)

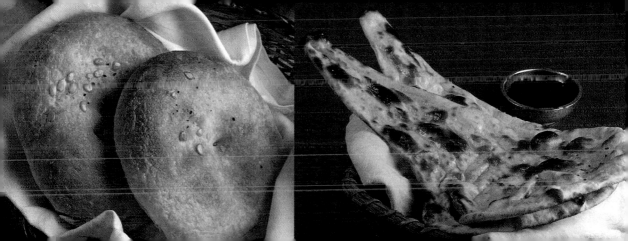

Boondi Raita
Crisp puffed gram flour pellets in yoghurt

Preparation time: 10 min.
Cooking time: 30 min.
Serves: 4

Accompaniments

Ingredients:

Gram flour (*besan*)	2½ tbsp / 30 gm
Salt	¼ tsp
Baking powder	2 gm
Water as required	
Refined oil for frying	
Yoghurt (*dahi*), whisked	4½ cups / 900 gm
Cumin (*jeera*) seeds, roasted, crushed	a pinch
Red chilli powder	1 tsp / 2 gm

Method:

1. Mix together gram flour, salt, and baking powder in a bowl; gradually add water and whisk to a smooth batter, having a consistency of heavy cream.

2. Heat the oil in a pan; pour about 2 tbsp batter at a time into a frying spoon with several holes. Hold the spoon above the pan and press the batter through the holes with your fingers. They will froth in the hot oil, then rise to the surface.

3. Fry until crisp and golden in colour. Remove, drain on paper towels. Repeat till all the batter is used.

4. In a bowl of warm water, put 2-3 tbsp of *boondi*, leave to soften, then gently squeeze between palms to remove excess water, keep aside.

5. Mix yoghurt with salt, and spices in a bowl until smooth and creamy. Stir in the soaked *boondi* and serve chilled as an accompaniment to any meal.

Pudina Raita
Mint in yoghurt

Ingredients:

Yoghurt (*dahi*)	3 cups / 600 gm
Salt to taste	
Mint (*pudina*) leaves, dried, crushed	5 tbsp / 20 gm
Cumin (*jeera*) powder	½ tsp

Method:

1. In a bowl, whisk yoghurt with salt and cumin powder.
2. Add the mint leaves.
3. Refrigerate for half an hour.
4. Sprinkle mint leaves (1 tbsp) and serve as an accompaniment to any dish.

Kheer

A rich creamy rice pudding

Preparation time: 1 hr.
Cooking time: 1 hr.
Serves: 4

Dessert

Ingredients:

Milk	5 cups / 1 lt
Ghee	2 tsp / 10 gm
Rice, long grain, washed, soaked for 1 hour	¼ cup / 50 gm
Sugar	½ cup / 75 gm
Green cardamom (*choti elaichi*) powder	1 tsp / 2 gm
Raisins (*kishmish*)	1 tbsp / 10 gm
Almonds (*badam*), blanched, slivered	1 tbsp / 15 gm
Saffron (*kesar*), dissolved in 2 tbsp milk	a few strands

Method:

1. Boil the milk in a pot. In another pot heat the ghee; add the rice and stir-fry for 4-5 minutes till it begins to brown lightly.
2. Add the milk and bring the mixture to the boil, stirring constantly to prevent the rice from sticking. Simmer till the rice is cooked.
3. Stir in the sugar. Simmer till the milk thickens.
4. Add the green cardamom powder, raisins and almonds.
5. Sprinkle the saffron and serve hot in winter and cold in summer.

Glossary of Cooking Terms

Baste — To moisten meat, poultry or game during roasting by spooning over it, its juices.

Batter — A mixture of flour, liquid and sometimes other ingredients, of a thin or thick consistency.

Blend — To mix two or more ingredients thoroughly together.

Coat — To cover food that is to be fried with flour, egg, and breadcrumbs, or batter.

Fry — To cook in hot fat or oil. In the case of shallow frying, only a small quantity of fat is used in a shallow pan. The food must be turned halfway through to cook both sides evenly. In the case of deep-frying, sufficient fat is used to cover the food completely.

Rub in — To incorporate the fat into flour, using the fingertips.

Sauté — To cook in an open pan in hot, shallow fat, tossing the food to prevent it from sticking.

Simmer — To boil gently on low heat.

Stir-fry — To fry rapidly while stirring and tossing.

Stock — Liquid produced when meat, poultry, bones, vegetables are simmered in water with herbs and flavourings for several hours.

Index

ISBN: 978-81-7436-296-4

© **This edition Roli & Janssen BV 2010**
Fifth impression
Published in India by Roli Books
in arrangement with Roli & Janssen BV
M-75, Greater Kailash II (Market), New Delhi-110 048, India
Tel.: ++91-11-40682000, Fax: ++91-11-29217185
E-mail: info@rolibooks.com, Website: www.rolibooks.com

Photographs: Dheeraj Paul and Deepak Budhraja

Printed and bound in Singapore